Scott Foresman

Scott Foresman

Reading

for Florida

Scott Foresman

About the Cover Artist

Maryjane Begin and her family live in Providence, Rhode Island, where she teaches college students when she is not working on her own art. Many of her illustrations—even imaginary places—show how things in Providence look.

ISBN 0-328-01974-7

Copyright © 2002, Pearson Education, Inc.

2 3 4 5 6 7 8 9 10 V063 10 09 08 07 06 05 04 03 02

Program Authors

Peter Afflerbach

James Beers

Camille Blachowicz

Candy Dawson Boyd

Wendy Cheyney

Deborah Diffily

Dolores Gaunty-Porter

Connie Juel

Donald Leu

Jeanne Paratore

Sam Sebesta

Karen Kring Wixson

Editorial Offices: Glenview, Illinois • Parsippany, New Jersey • New York, New York
Sales Offices: Parsippany, New Jersey • Duluth, Georgia • Glenview, Illinois
Carrollton, Texas • Ontario, California

Contents

Favorite Things Old and New

Unit 4

Favorite Things Old and New

How do things get to be favorites?

The Red Stone Game

by Mary Blount Christian
illustrated by Elizabeth Allen

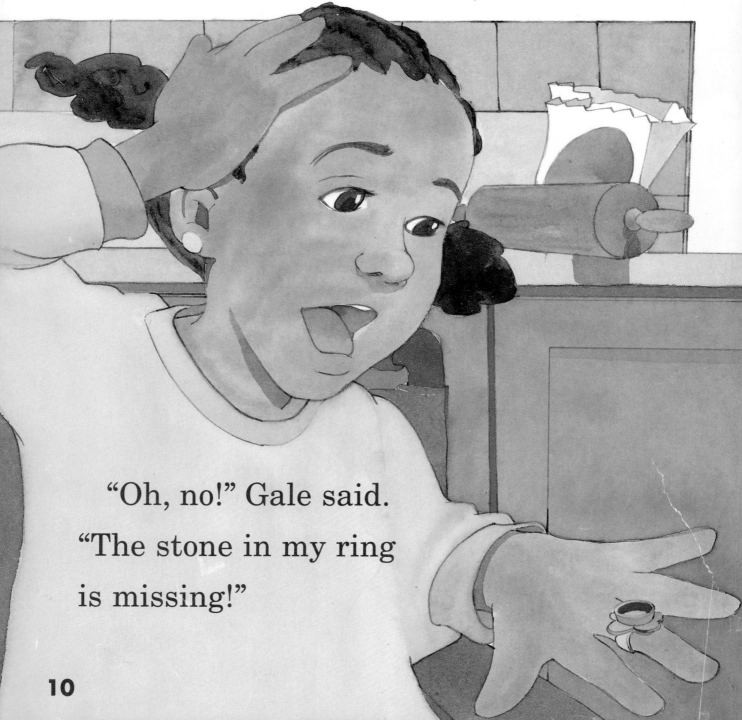

"Oh, no!" Gale said.
"The stone in my ring
is missing!"

Nate and Pam came in.

"Did you call us?" they asked.

"I have to find my stone,"

said Gale.

"We just made cookies with Mom," said Nate. "Did you have it before we made cookies?"

"Yes," said Gale.

"Did you have it after we made cookies?" Pam asked.

"No," Gale said.

"It must be someplace!
Let's play a game called Find
the Red Stone," said Pam.

Nate looked on the floor.
Pam looked in the sink. Gale
looked in the pan.

Something made Gale laugh.

She picked up a cookie.

"I see something," she said.

"The face of this cookie has a red nose!" said Gale. Gale, Nate, and Pam laughed as they all ate cookies. No one ate the cookie with the red nose!

The Gingerbread Man

retold by Sally Bell

illustrated by Bob Barner

A woman and a man
lived on a farm.
The woman said,
"I will make a
gingerbread man."
So she did.

Soon she heard something.
She looked.
The gingerbread man jumped out.

The woman wanted to catch him.
The man wanted to catch him.
But the gingerbread man ran away.

The gingerbread man ran fast.

He laughed.

He sang,

"Run, run, as fast as you can.

You can not catch me.

I am the gingerbread man!"

He saw a man.

23

"Stop!" called the man.

"I want something to eat.

You look good."

The gingerbread man ran on.

The man ran after him.

The gingerbread man laughed.

He sang,

"Run, run, as fast as you can.

You can not catch me.

I am the gingerbread man!"

"Stop!" called the girl.
"I want something to eat.
You look good."
The gingerbread man ran on.
The girl ran after him.

The gingerbread man laughed.
He sang,
"Run, run, as fast as you can.
You can not catch me.
I am the gingerbread man!"

He saw a boy.

"Stop!" called the boy.

"I want something to eat.

You look good."

The gingerbread man ran on.

The boy ran after him.

The gingerbread man laughed.

He sang,

"Run, run, as fast as you can.

You can not catch me.

I am the gingerbread man!"

The gingerbread man saw water.

He stopped.

He did not know what to do.

The gingerbread man saw a fox.

The fox saw him.

The gingerbread man sang,
"Run, run, as fast as you can.
You can not catch me.
I am the gingerbread man!"

The fox said, "I do not want
to catch you.
I will help you.
You can ride on me."

The gingerbread man got
on the fox.
The fox jumped into the water.
The fox said,
"You will get wet.
Ride on my head."
The gingerbread man did.

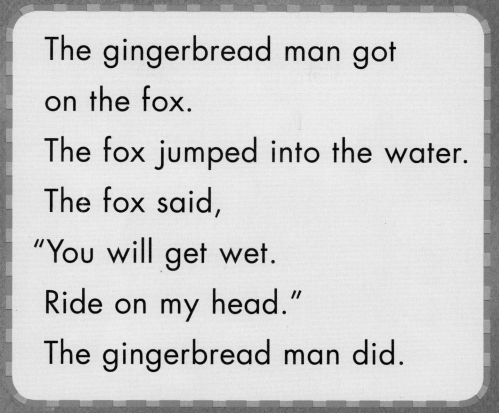

The fox said,
"You will get wet.
Ride on my nose."
The gingerbread man did.
The fox put his head up.
The gingerbread man fell.

Snap!
The fox ate him up.
And that was the end
of the gingerbread man.

About the Illustrator

Bob Barner uses special papers to make his pictures. He cuts and tears the papers just the way he wants them. Then he glues them down. He finishes his work with pencils and pastels. For this story, he made a clay gingerbread man. The clay made it look like a real cookie.

Mr. Barner says, "The fox is my favorite character in this story. I like the way he looks."

Read Together

Reader Response

Let's Talk

If you were in this story, who would you like to be? Why?

Let's Think

What does the fox do that tells you he is clever?

 **FCAT**

Let's Write

What if the gingerbread man got away from the fox? What might he do next? Write a new ending for the story. Draw a picture for your ending.

Make a Gingerbread Man

Use your gingerbread man to retell the story.

What you need:

brown paper   paper or tissue

scissors   glue or stapler

What you do:

1. Fold a piece of brown paper in half.
2. Draw an outline of the gingerbread man.
3. Cut along the lines.
4. Staple or glue almost all the way around.
5. Stuff the gingerbread man with newspaper or tissue.
6. Close up the opening.
7. Draw the face and buttons.

Use your gingerbread man to retell the story.

Language Arts

Verbs

A **verb** tells what a person, animal, or thing does. Many verbs are action words.

The boy **shakes** the sprinkles. The cat **licks** the milk.

What words tell the action?

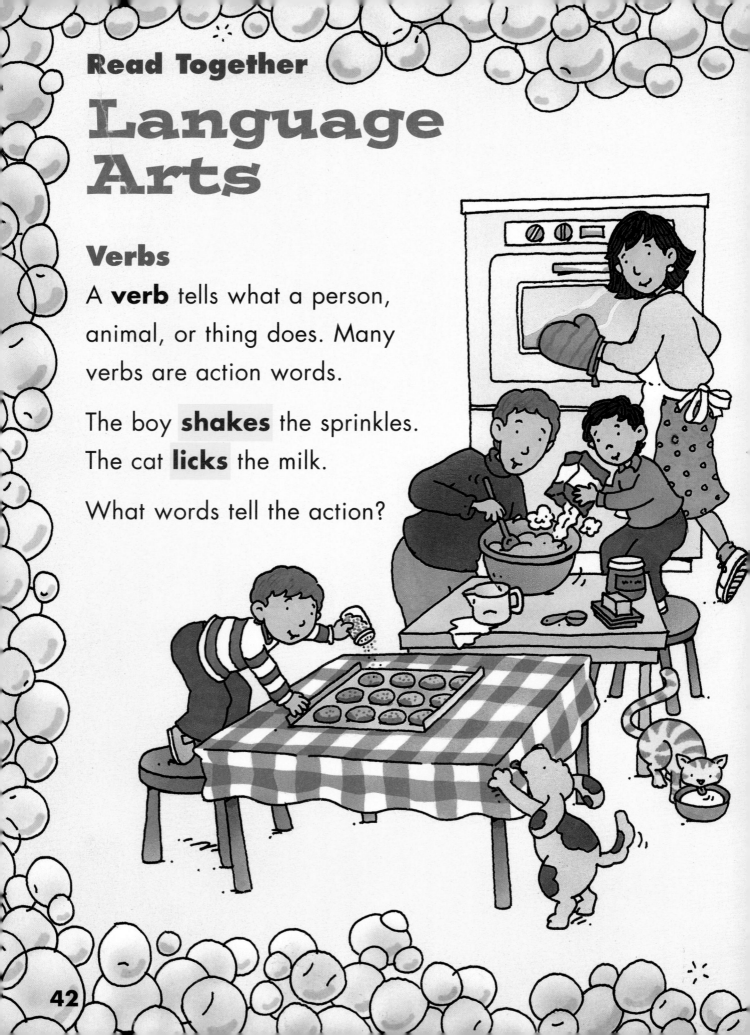

Talk

Look at the pictures. Tell what the people, animals, and things do.

Write

Write the sentences. Draw a line under the action verbs.

1. **The little boy pours flour.**
2. **Mother opens the oven door.**
3. **The dog wags its tail.**

Write your own sentences. Use verbs that tell action. Draw a line under the action verbs.

The Same as You

by Sharon Fear

illustrated by Stacey Schuett

"Grandpa? Was Mother like me when she was little?" asked Katie.

"Yes, she was," said Grandpa. "Your mother was brave. She liked to jump into the water. The same as you."

"Your mother got good grades. She made all of us proud every day. The same as you."

"Grandpa? Was Grandmother like me?" asked Katie.

"Yes, she was," said Grandpa.

"Your grandmother was thin. She had thick, black hair. Her name was Katie. The same as you."

"Your grandmother liked to bake. She made cakes like this. She made all of us laugh every day. The same as you."

"Grandpa? Am I like you?" asked Katie.

"Oh, no," said Grandpa. "I am the checkers champ. No one plays checkers like me! I plan to win every game."

"Oh, Grandpa!" said Katie. "I plan to win every game too. One day I *will* be the same as you."

Cherry Pies
and Lullabies

by Lynn Reiser

Contents

1. Cherry Pies

My great-grandmother
baked a cherry pie
for my grandmother.

My grandmother
baked a cherry pie
for my mother.

My mother
baked a cherry pie
for me.

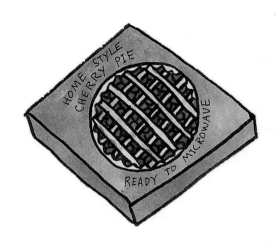

And I
baked a cherry pie
for my bear.

Every time it was
the same, but different.

2. Flowers

My great-grandmother
made a crown of flowers
for my grandmother.

My grandmother
made a crown of flowers
for my mother.

My mother made
a crown of flowers
for me.

And I made
a crown of flowers
for my bear.

Every time it was
the same, but different.

3. Quilts

My great-grandmother
gave a quilt
to my grandmother.

My grandmother
gave a quilt
to my mother.

My mother
gave a quilt
to me.

And
I gave a quilt
to my bear.

Every time it was the same, but different.

4. Lullabies

My great-grandmother
sang a lullaby
to my grandmother.

My grandmother
sang a lullaby
to my mother.

My mother
sang a lullaby
to me.

I sang
a lullaby
to my bear.

And every time
it was the same.

Lullaby

words by Lynn Reiser

music by Johannes Brahms

Lul - la- by and good-night. Pie is   sweet, stars are

bright.__   Close your eyes__ un- til   day. ___   In your

dreams__laugh and   play. Crowned with flow-   ers you

sleep,__wrapped in love soft and   deep.__ Close your

eyes__ now and   stay__wrapped in love un- til   day.

About the Author and Illustrator

Lynn Reiser

Cherry Pies and Lullabies is about Lynn Reiser's family. The people in her family have lived in different places. Her grandmother lived on a farm. Her mother lived in a small town. Ms. Reiser lived in a suburb. Now Ms. Reiser has a niece who lives in a city.

Lynn Reiser says that life has changed for her family, but some things "like lullabies, are always the same."

Reader Response

Let's Talk

Pretend you are the girl in the story. What gift would you make for the bear?

Let's Think

Four people gave gifts in the story. How are the gifts the same? How are they different?

FCAT

Let's Write

Look back at the Contents on page 53. These things are special to the girl. What is special to you? Write how to make it.

Make a Treasure Box

Make a box to keep special things in.

What you need:

shoe box	colored paper
scissors	glue or stapler
buttons	string

What you do:

Glue paper cutouts on your shoe box.

Add art and other things to your shoe box.

Collect your special things. Put them in the box.

Language Arts

Verbs for One

Verbs may tell what one person, animal, or thing does. Add **-s** to these verbs.

My uncle **plays** the piano. Grandmother **sings**.

Talk

Look at the picture. Tell what each person, animal, or thing does.

Write

Write the sentences. Circle the verbs
that tell what one person does.

1. **Uncle Joe wears brown shoes.**
2. **Grandmother holds the music.**
3. **The boy claps.**

Write your own sentences. Tell what one
person, animal, or thing does. Circle
the verbs.

Rose and Grandma Make the Sun Shine

by Juanita Havill

illustrated by
Darryl Ligasan

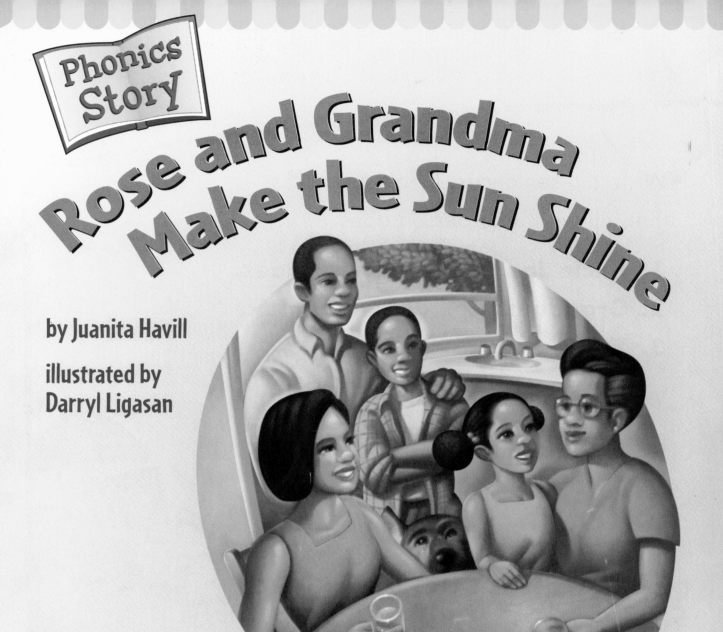

"Where can we go for our

family picnic?" Grandma said.

"Lone Lake!" said Rose and

Kevin and their mother and father.

"Everybody has to help," Dad
said. "I'll shop for things to eat."
"I'm going to make cakes,"
said Mom.

"I'll call the rest of the family," said Kevin.

"I'm going to play games with the little kids," said Rose.

She wrote a list of things to do.

"What are you going to do, Grandma?" said Rose.

"I'll think of something," said Grandma.

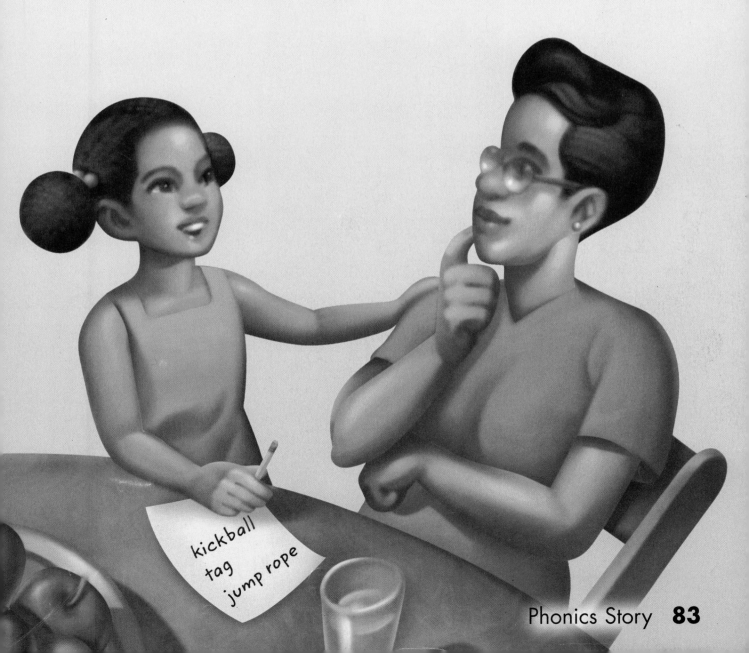

The family went to Lone Lake.

"Look at those clouds," said Kevin.

"We'll have to go home."

"No, we don't. I have a plan,"
Grandma said.

"Who has stories to tell?" said
Grandma.

"I have one," said Rose.

The family sat close by the stove.

They all had a turn. After a
while, the sun shone.

"Thank you, Grandma," said
Rose. "You had a very good plan."

"Our stories made the sun
shine," said Grandma.

Our Family Get-Together

by Carmen Tafolla and
Israel Tafolla Bernal

Last fall we had a big family
get-together. My father had the idea.
But it was my idea too.

Everyone came to the same place at the same time. They came to my uncle's ranch in Texas. Then we just had fun together.

Some came by car.
Some came by plane.
Uncle Richard just walked.
The get-together was at
his ranch.

There were so many cousins at the get-together. There were brothers, sisters, fathers, mothers, uncles, aunts, and grandmothers!

All of us came with something. My father came with hot dogs. My uncle came with a watermelon. And what did I come with?

My best joke!

Uncle Richard has
horses on his ranch.
He has cows and
sheep too.

Grandma showed us an old picture. It was Grandpa's father. He had on a hat and rode a horse.

I rode a horse too.

My father held the rope.

My mother took a picture of me.

I was going to look like

Grandpa's father!

I met a new cousin.

Ronnie was six like me.

He liked jokes too.

We looked for frogs.

And we saw a lot of them!

The frogs went up a
tree very fast.

They were very little.

My cousin saw three.

I saw five.

We saw more than frogs.

We saw a big fence and

two very old wheels.

Late in the day, my sister and my cousin put on a show. It was sunny, so we sat in the shade.

Mother made a family tree.
A family tree shows all the
names in the family.
Here is my name.

We didn't want the fun to stop.

But it was time to go home.

"Thank you for this get-together,"

said Mother. "I hope we'll see you

again soon."

I didn't know my family was so big.

I met a new cousin. It was fun to
look for frogs with him. Next year,
I will find more frogs!

I bet next year I will find
more cousins too.

About the Authors

Carmen Tafolla wrote this story together with her son, Israel. It tells about their family get-together at a ranch near San Antonio, Texas. Dr. Tafolla and her son wrote this story as if only Israel were speaking.

At the get-together, Israel really did meet a new cousin. And he met some frogs too!

Four Generations

by Mary Ann Hoberman

Sometimes when we go out for walks,
I listen while my father talks.

The thing he talks of most of all
Is how it was when he was small

And he went walking with *his* dad
And conversations that they had

About *his* father and the talks
They had when *they* went out for walks.

Reader Response

Let's Talk

Pretend you went to a family get-together. What would you want to do?

Let's Think

Look back at the two stories. Both are about family get-togethers. What did the families do that was the same? What did they do that was different?

 **FCAT**

Let's Write

The Tafolla family get-together was at a ranch. Where would you like your family to have a get-together? Tell why.

Make an Invitation

Make an invitation to a family get-together.

1. Fold a piece of paper in half.

2. On the outside, draw a picture and write Please Come.

3. On the inside, tell people where the get-together will be. Tell them the date and time.

Please Come

Language Arts

Verbs for Two or More

Verbs may tell what two or more
people, animals, or things do.
Do not add **-s** to these verbs.

The children **eat**.

The men **bring** the food.

Talk

Look at the pictures. Tell what two or more people, animals, and things do.

Write

Write the sentences. Circle the verbs that tell what two or more people, animals, or things do.

1. **Babies play on the mat.**
2. **Squirrels run in the grass.**
3. **The girls ride on the horse.**

Write your own sentences. Tell what two or more people, animals, or things do. Circle the verbs.

The Rolling Rice Cake
A Story from Japan

retold by Eric A. Kimmel   illustrated by Oki S. Han

An old man was going to cut wood. His wife made pretty rice cakes for him.

"Thank you," the old man said. "You make the best rice cakes!"

The old man cut lots of wood. Soon he wanted a rice cake. The rice cake fell out of his hand. It rolled down a hole.

The old man looked down. He
heard a pretty song.

"Rolling rice cake is so nice.
Roll a cake to your friends
the mice!"

It was a family of mice.
"Sing again!" the old man
said. He rolled down his rice
cakes. The mice sang as
they ate them.

The old man wanted to be closer. He wanted to hear the singing better. He fell into the hole and rolled to the bottom.

"Nice old man," the mice said. "Here is a present. A little bag of rice."

"Thank you," the old man said. "Can you help me out of this hole?"

The mice sang this song.

"Rolling old man is so nice.
We'll help our friend.
He fed the mice."

Soon the mice rolled the
old man out of the hole!

The old man took the rice
bag home. The man and his
wife never ran out of rice.
There was always lots of rice
to make rice cakes for all.

The Rat and the Cat

by Edward
Marshall

illustrated by
James Marshall

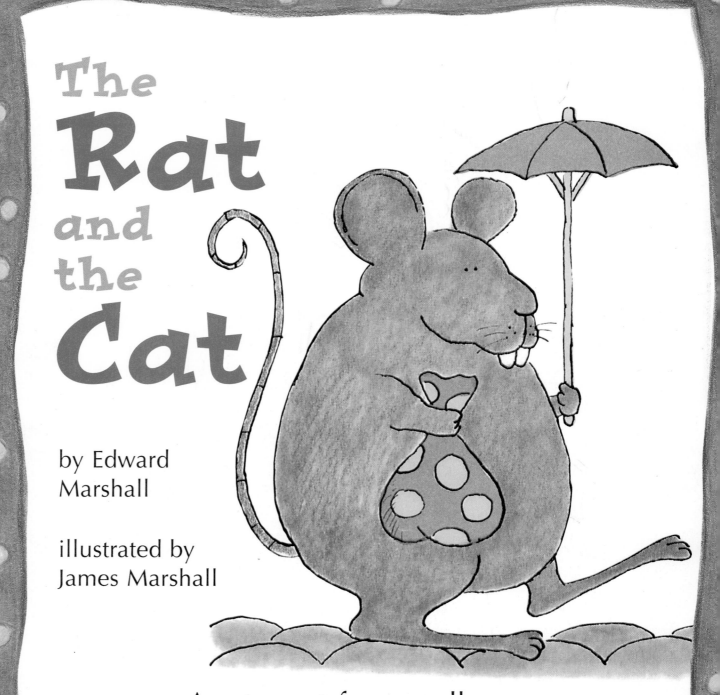

A rat went for a walk.

"What a fine day," he said.

"The sun is shining
and all is well."

Soon he came to a shop.

"My, my," said the rat.

"What a pretty cat.

And I have never had a cat."

"I will buy that cat
and have a friend," he said.
And he went into the shop.
"I want a cat," he said.

"Are you sure you want a *cat?*"
asked the owner.

"I am sure," said the rat.
"And I want that one."

"That will be ten cents,"
said the man.
"If you are *sure.*"

"I am sure," said the rat.
"Here is my last dime.
Give me my cat."

The rat and the cat left the shop.

"We will be friends," said the rat.

"Do you think so?" said the cat.

"Well, we'll see."

The rat and the cat sat
in the sun.
"What do you do for fun?"
asked the rat.

"I like to catch things,"
said the cat.

"That's nice," said the rat.

"I am hungry," said the cat.
"How about lunch?"

"A fine idea," said the rat.
"What is your favorite dish?"

"I do not want to say,"
said the cat.

"You can tell me," said the rat.
"We are friends."

"Are you *sure* you want to
know?" said the cat.

"I am sure," said the rat.
"Tell me what you like to eat."

"I will tell you," said the cat.
"But let us go where
we can be alone."

"Fine with me," said the rat.

The cat and the rat
went to the beach.
"I know," said the rat. "Fish.
You like to eat fish."

"Not at all," said the cat.
"It's much better than fish."

"Tell me," said the rat.
"I just *have* to know."

"Come closer," said the cat.
"And I will tell you."

"Yes?" said the rat.

"What I like," said the cat, "is . . ."

". . . CHEESE! I love cheese!"

"So do I," said the rat.
"And I have some here."

"Hooray!" said the cat.
"And now we are friends."

So they sat on the beach
and ate the cheese.

And that was that.

About the Author and Illustrator

Edward Marshall and James Marshall were the same person! James Marshall's middle name was Edward. Sometimes he used the name James. Other times he used the name Edward. For "The Rat and the Cat" he used both names!

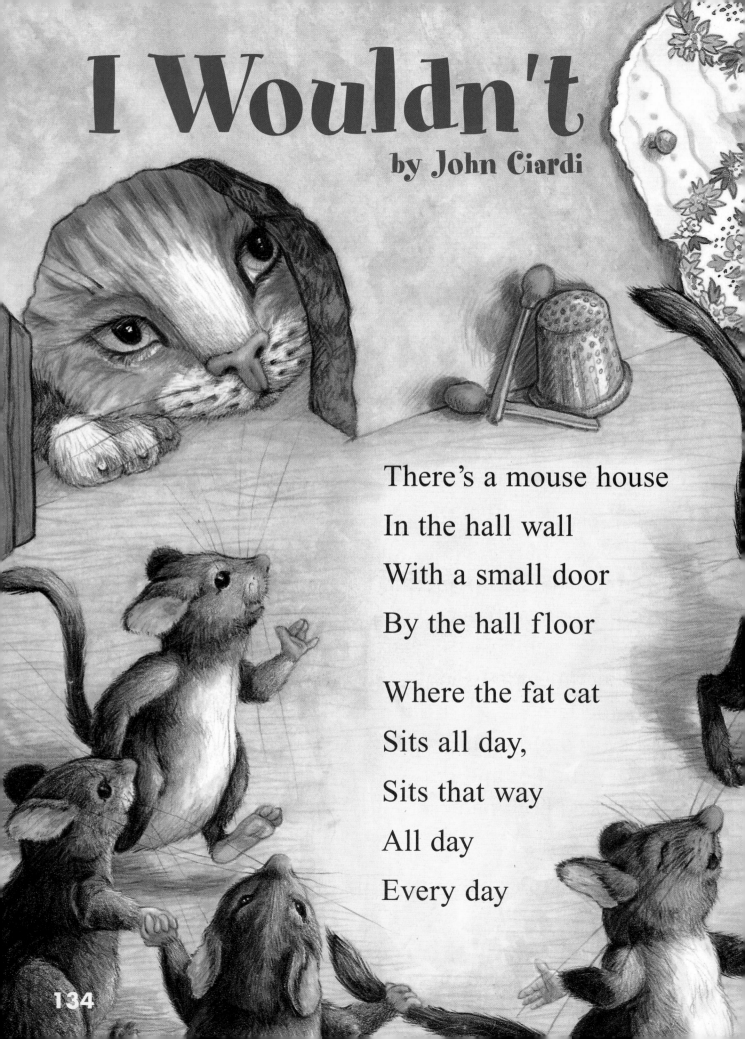

I Wouldn't

by John Ciardi

There's a mouse house

In the hall wall

With a small door

By the hall floor

Where the fat cat

Sits all day,

Sits that way

All day

Every day

Just to say,
"Come out and play"
To the nice mice
In the mouse house
In the hall wall
With the small door
By the hall floor.

And do they
Come out and play
When the fat cat
Asks them to?

Well, would you?

Reader Response

Let's Talk

If you were a rat, would you buy a cat for a pet? Why or why not?

Let's Think

What did you think would happen in the story? Were you surprised? Was the rat surprised? Tell why or why not.

 **FCAT**

Let's Write

You are the cat. Write a friendly letter to the rat. Tell the rat how you feel about him.

Make a Calendar

The cat and the rat went to the beach.
What other things can they do?
Make a calendar for a week.

1. Work with six classmates. Each of you pick a day of the week.

2. Write the name of your day at the top of a piece of paper.

3. Draw a picture of something the cat and the rat can do that day.

4. Tape your pictures together to show a week of fun for the new friends.

Language Arts

Verbs for Now and for the Past

Verbs can tell about action that takes place now.

Verbs can tell about action that happened in the past. Add **–ed** to the verb.

The children **mix** the lemonade.

The children **mixed** the lemonade.

Talk

Tell about things you see people doing in the pictures.

Write

Write the sentences.

Draw one line under verbs that tell about now.

Draw two lines under verbs that tell about the past.

1. **The woman mowed the grass.**
2. **The girl jumps rope.**
3. **A man washed his car.**
4. **The dog barks.**

Write your own sentences. Use verbs for now and for the past.

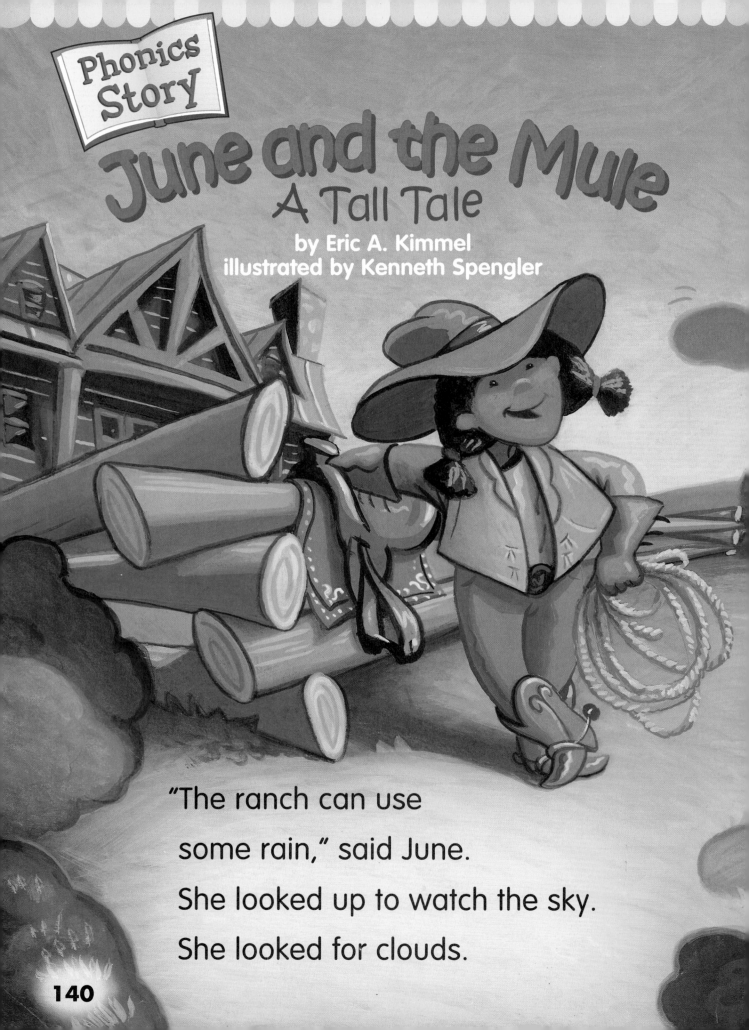

June and the Mule
A Tall Tale

by Eric A. Kimmel
illustrated by Kenneth Spengler

"The ranch can use
some rain," said June.
She looked up to watch the sky.
She looked for clouds.

A funny cloud came by.

There were four legs on the cloud.

There were long ears on it.

It looked like a mule.

"I think I can catch it," June said.

She flung her rope.

That rope went a long, long way.

June got the mule.

The funny mule bucked.
He jumped and kicked.
June used her rope to pull
the mule down.

June jumped on the mule.
She rode with him in the sky.
June took out her flute.
"I'll play a tune for the mule!"
she said.

Then June sang,

"Cute mule, funny mule,

Make the sky clang and bang!

Ring! Ding! Make it rain!

Drop by drop! Inch by inch!"

The mule kicked both back legs.
His kicks made thunder crash
and lightning flash.
He made rain fall from the sky.

The rain ended.

The mule wanted to stay with June.

"Stick around," she said.

"I'll call you Jules!"

Slim, Luke, and the Mules

by Stewart Christopher

illustrated by Wendy Shaul

Slim and Luke were cowboys
a long time ago.

They lived on a big ranch.

The ranch was a long way from town.

Slim and Luke had five mules.

One day Slim said,
"We are out of food.
We have to go to town.
We can use the mules to
bring the food home."

Slim and Luke lined up the mules.
Slim got on the mule at the
front of the line.
Luke got on the mule at the
end of the line.

Luke said, "How will we get all five
mules to town? We may lose one."

Slim said, "You watch the mules.
That way we will not lose one."

The cowboys left for town with the mules.

Soon Slim looked back at Luke. Slim said, "Are all five mules here?"

Luke said, "I think so. I have been watching them the whole time. I will count them."

Luke pointed at the mules in line in front of him. He counted,

"One mule,
two mules,
three mules,
four mules."

"Four mules!" said Luke.

"That's funny.

I have been watching the mules.

How did we lose one?

I will count them again."

Luke counted the mules in
front of him again.

He counted four mules.

"We *have* lost a mule," he said.

Slim said, "I will count the mules."
Slim pointed at the mules in line in
back of him. He counted,

"One mule,
two mules,
three mules,
four mules."

Then he said,
"Luke, I counted four mules too.
We have lost a mule.
We have to find it."

The cowboys got down and
began to look.
They both looked and looked
for that lost mule.
But they didn't find it.
At last Luke said, "That mule
must be lost for good."

Slim said, "Let's go back and
count the mules again.
Maybe more mules are
lost by now."

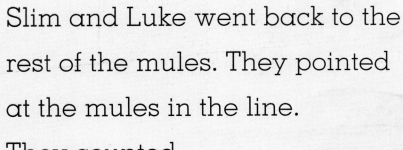

Slim and Luke went back to the
rest of the mules. They pointed
at the mules in the line.
They counted,

"One mule,
two mules,
three mules,
four mules,
five mules."

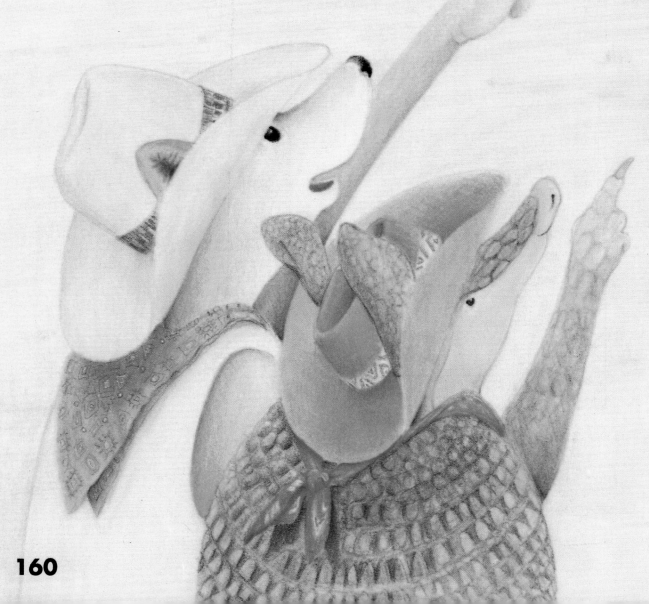

Slim said, "What do you know!
The lost mule is back."

Then Luke said, "Now we can
go to town."

And that's what they did.

Slim and Luke's Animals

These are the animals on Slim and Luke's ranch.

mules   horses   cattle   pigs

This bar graph also shows how many animals Slim and Luke have.

Animals on Slim and Luke's Ranch										
mules	■	■	■	■	■					
horses	■	■	■	■	■	■	■			
cattle	■	■	■	■	■	■	■	■	■	
pigs	■	■	■	■						
	1	2	3	4	5	6	7	8	9	10

Let's Talk

Which animals do they have the most of?
Which animals do they have the fewest of?

About the Illustrator

Wendy Shaul grew up in the Southwest. She loves snakes, lizards, and other critters. She also loves art, so she put her two interests together. Now she's an artist who often draws animals.

Ms. Shaul saw her first armadillo in Costa Rica. She remembered it when she drew Luke for this story.

Reader Response

Let's Talk

Look back in the story. What do the pictures tell you about where Slim and Luke live? Would you like to live there?

Let's Think

Did Slim and Luke really lose a mule? How did they find it?

 FCAT

Let's Write

The story pictures show the mules on the way to town. Draw a picture of the mules on the way home from town. Write a sentence about your picture.

Readers Theater

Read and act out the story
as a play.

1. One person reads what
Slim says.

2. One person reads what Luke says.

3. Two people play Slim and Luke.

4. Five people play the mules.

Language Arts

Is, Are, Was, Were

Use **is** and **are** to
tell about now.

Beth **is** on a horse.
The trails **are** bumpy.

Use **was** and **were**
to tell about the past.

Marta's horse **was** tired.
The other horses **were**
at the ranch.

Talk

Look at the pictures. Use **is, are, was,** and **were** to tell what you see.

Write

Write the sentences. Draw one line under verbs that tell about now. Draw two lines under verbs that tell about the past.

1. **The horses are in the barn now.**
2. **The sky is blue.**
3. **The sky was gray yesterday.**
4. **The horses were in the field.**

Write your own sentences. Use **is** and **are** to tell about now. Use **was** and **were** to tell about the past.

Riddle-dee Fiddle-dee-dee

by Helen Lester
illustrated by Laura Ovresat

He, She, and Me

Up in a tree

Playing with riddles

Fiddle-dee-dee.

168

173

He, She, and Me
Up in a tree
Playing with riddles
Fiddle-dee-dee!

175

The Riddles

by Bernard Wiseman

Boris the Bear met Morris the Moose.

"Do you like riddles?" Boris asked.

Morris asked, "How do they taste?"

Boris said, "You do not eat riddles."

Morris asked, "Do you drink them?"

Boris said, "You do not eat riddles.

You do not drink riddles. You ask them!

Listen—I will ask you a riddle."

Boris asked, "What has four feet—"

Morris yelled, "ME!"

"I did not finish," Boris said.

"What has four feet and a tail—"

"ME!" Morris yelled.

"I still did not finish!" Boris cried.

"Let me finish!"

Morris put a hoof over his mouth.

Boris asked, "What has four feet and a tail and flies?"

"ME!" Morris yelled. "I have four feet and a tail, and flies come and sit on me all the time!"

"No, no!" Boris growled.

"The answer is: A horse in an airplane!

"Here is another riddle. What kind of comb cannot comb hair?"

"I know!" Morris cried.

"A broken comb!"

"NO! NO! NO!" Boris shouted.
"The answer is a honeycomb!"

"What is a honeycomb?"
Morris asked.

Boris said, "It is the inside
of a bee house. Don't you
know anything?"

Morris said, "I know about riddles.
You do not eat riddles. You do not drink
riddles. You ASK riddles."

Boris said, "And you must answer them!

Try to answer this riddle.

What kind of bee does not sting?"

"I know!" cried Morris.

"A friendly bee!"

"NO! NO!" Boris yelled.

Morris cried, "A sleeping bee!"

"NO! NO! NO!" Boris shouted.

"The answer is: a beetle. Oh, you don't know how to answer the riddles. I am not going to ask you any more."

Morris said, "You know how to answer riddles. Let me ask you riddles."

"Go ahead," said Boris. "Ask me riddles."

Morris asked, "What has four feet and a tail and flies?"

Boris answered, "A horse in an airplane."

"No! No!" Morris cried. "A moose in an airplane."

Boris yelled, "You mean a HORSE!"

Morris said, "I mean a moose. I want a moose to get an airplane ride!"

Then Morris said, "Here is another riddle. What kind of beetle does not sting?"

Boris said, "You mean, what kind of BEE does not sting!"

Morris laughed. "I mean what kind of beetle! All bees sting!"

Boris shouted, "Oh, you don't
know anything about riddles!
I am going home!"

A bird asked Morris, "What is
he angry about?"

"Riddles," said Morris. "He
does not like them."

About the Author and Illustrator

Bernard Wiseman said, "I was a cartoonist long before I was a writer." He began drawing cartoons when he was a young sailor.

Mr. Wiseman wrote funny children's books. He said that they were like his cartoons. If you like funny books, you might enjoy reading other books about Morris and Boris.

Reader Response

Let's Talk

Would you rather ask riddles like Boris or answer riddles like Morris? Tell why.

Let's Think

Why was Boris so angry with Morris?

FCAT
Let's Write

Morris told the bird that Boris went home because he didn't like riddles. Tell why you think Boris went home.

Have a Riddle Quiz

A riddle is a puzzle that asks a question.
Follow these steps to write a riddle.
Then have a Riddle Quiz with your class.

First, think of what
you will write about.

Next, write clues about
it and ask *What am I?*

3 Last, ask your riddles in a Riddle Quiz.

Language Arts

Using the Word *Not*

The word **not** changes what a sentence means.

Rose is talking.   Ana is **not** talking.

A verb and the word **not** can be put together. They make a shorter word called a **contraction**. The letter **o** is left out of the word **not**. An **'** is used in place of the letter **o**.

is n**o**t = isn't   was n**o**t = wasn't

are n**o**t = aren't   were n**o**t = weren't

Talk

Look at the pictures. Tell who is and who is not doing something. Use contractions.

Write

Write the sentences. Change the meaning. Add **not**.

1. **Jenny is sewing.**
2. **Tom and Sam are talking.**

Write the sentences. Use contractions.

3. **Angelo was not painting this morning.**
4. **Ana and Rose were not in school yesterday.**

Write two of your own sentences. Use a verb and the word **not** in the first sentence. Put the verb and the word **not** together in the second sentence. Use an **'**.

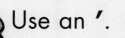

The Same as You
Cherry Pies and Lullabies

every

made

mother

of

was

The Red Stone Game
The Gingerbread Man

after

as

call

catch

laugh

something

Rose and Grandma Make the Sun Shine
Our Family Get-Together

father

going

has

thank

very

June and the Mule

Slim, Luke, and the Mules

count
four
funny
long
watch
were

The Rolling Rice Cake

The Rat and the Cat

be
friend
pretty
soon
your

Riddle-dee Fiddle-dee-dee

The Riddles

about
answer
any
ask
kind
over

FCAT Talk

Use Pictures

A test may ask you to look at a picture or pictures to answer a question.

A test about *Our Family Get-Together* might show you this picture and ask this question.

1. Where did the family get-together take place?

Ⓐ beach

Ⓑ ranch

Ⓒ cowboy

Read the question. Look for clues in the picture. Which answer seems right?

Here is how one boy figured out his answer.

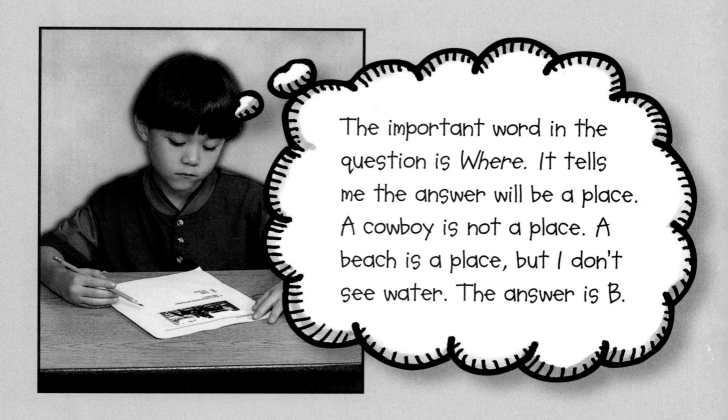

The important word in the question is *Where*. It tells me the answer will be a place. A cowboy is not a place. A beach is a place, but I don't see water. The answer is B.

Try it!

Look at this picture from *Our Family Get-Together*. Read the question. Use clues in the picture to tell which answer is right.

2. Who came to the family get-together?

(A) only children

(B) only grandparents

(C) the whole family

Glossary

Words from Your Stories

Aa

alone   **Alone** means without anyone else.

angry   When you are upset and mad about something, you are **angry**. Dad was **angry** when I broke the window.

angry

answer   To **answer** means to speak or write something when you are asked a question. Who will **answer** the question?

answer

Bb

before   Your turn comes **before** mine. Have you been to the zoo **before?**

Cc

catch   **Catch** means to take and hold something moving.

count   **Count** means to add up or find the number of something.

cousins   Your **cousins** are the children of any of your uncles or aunts.

cowboys   **Cowboys** are men who work on a cattle ranch or perform in rodeos.

Dd _____

different   **Different** means not alike. The dogs are all **different**.

different

Gg _____

growled   When an animal has **growled**, it has made a deep, angry sound.

Hh _____

heard   When the dog **heard** the sound, it began to bark.

hoof   A **hoof** is the hard part of the foot of some animals. Horses, cattle, sheep, and pigs have **hooves**.

hooray   **Hooray** is a shout of happiness.

hooray

Ii _____

idea   An **idea** is a thought or plan.

205

Ll

lightning **Lightning** is a flash of light in the sky.

lightning

lose When you **lose** something, you are not able to find it.

lullaby A **lullaby** is a soft song that quiets a baby so that it falls asleep.

Pp

pointed If you **pointed** to something, you showed it to someone using your finger.

proud **Proud** means thinking well of yourself or others.

pointed

Qq

quilt A **quilt** is a soft cover for a bed.

quilt

Rr

ranch A **ranch** is a very large farm and its buildings. Sheep, cattle, and horses are raised on **ranches**.

riddles   **Riddles** are puzzles that ask a question.

Ss

shining   When something is **shining**, it is giving off a bright light. The sun is **shining**.

shining

shouted   **Shouted** means called or yelled loudly.

stories   **Stories** tell about people and places and what happens to them.

Tt

thunder   **Thunder** is the loud noise that often follows lightning.

town   A **town** is a large group of houses and other buildings.

Ww

wears   When a person **wears** something, he or she has it on his or her body. The team **wears** matching baseball caps.

wears

wood   The trunk and branches of a tree are made of **wood**.

Tested Word List

The Red Stone Game
The Gingerbread Man

after
as
call
catch
laugh
something

The Same as You
Cherry Pies and Lullabies

every
made
mother
of
was

Rose and Grandma Make the Sun Shine
Our Family Get-Together

father
going
has
thank
very

The Rolling Rice Cake
The Rat and the Cat

be
friend
pretty
soon
your

June and the Mule: A Tall Tale
Slim, Luke, and the Mules

count
four
funny
long
watch
were

Riddle-dee Fiddle-dee-dee
The Riddles

about
answer
any
ask
kind
over

Acknowledgments

Text

Page 18: Adapted abridgment of *The Gingerbread Man* retold by Sally Bell. © 1985 Golden Books Publishing Company, Inc. Used by permission. All rights reserved.
Page 52: *Cherry Pies and Lullabies* by Lynn Reiser, pp. 6–38. Copyright © 1998 by Lynn Whisnant Reiser. Used with the permission of Greenwillow Books, an imprint of HarperCollins Publishers.
Page 105: "Four Generations" from *Fathers, Mothers, Sisters, Brothers* by Mary Ann Hoberman, p. 5. Text copyright © 1991 by Mary Ann Hoberman. Reprinted by permission of Little, Brown and Company.
Page 118: Abridgment of "Sam's Story" from *Three by the Sea* by Edward Marshall, pictures by James Marshall, pp. 20–34. Text copyright © 1981 by Edward Marshall. Pictures copyright © 1981 by James Marshall. Reprinted by permission of Dial Books for Young Readers, a division of Penguin Putnam, Inc.
Page 134: "I Wouldn't" from *You Read to Me, I'll Read to You* by John Ciardi. Reprinted by permission of the Ciardi Family.
Page 176: "The Riddles" from *Morris and Boris, Three Stories* by Bernard Wiseman. Reprinted by permission of Susan N. Wiseman.

Artists

Maryjane Begin, cover, 8–9
Elizabeth Allen, 10–17
Bob Barner, 18–39
Patrick Girouard, 40–43
Stacey Schuett, 44–51
Lynn Reiser, 52–75
Lori Osiecki, 76–79, 106–107
Darryl Ligasan, 80–87
Francisco X. Mora, 105
Marta Aviles, 108–109
Oki S. Han, 110–117
Pamela Paulsrud, (calligraphy) 110
James Marshall, 118–133
Paige Miglio, 134–135
Jason Wolff, 136–139
Kenneth Spengler, 140–147
Wendy Shaul, 148–167, 200–201
Laura Ovresat, 168–175
Janet Ocwieja, (props) 168
Bernard Wiseman, 176–195
Franklin Hammond, 196–199

Photographs

Every effort has been made to secure permission and provide appropriate credit for photographic material. The publisher deeply regrets any omission and pledges to correct errors called to their attention in subsequent editions.

Unless otherwise acknowledged, all photographs are the property of Scott Foresman, a division of Pearson Education. Page abbreviations are as follows: (t) top, (b) bottom, (l) left, (r) right, (ins) inset, (s) spot, (bk) background.
Page 39 Courtesy Bob Barner
Page 75 Courtesy Lynn Reiser, Photo: Branka Whisnant
Pages 88–104 Jim Markham for Scott Foresman
Page 133 Courtesy Houghton Mifflin Co.
Page 163 Courtesy Wendy Shaul
Page 195 Courtesy Susan Wiseman

Glossary

The contents of this glossary have been adapted from *My First Dictionary*. Copyright © 2000 by Scott Foresman and Company, a division of Addison Wesley Educational Publishers, Inc.